Volty

Practical Engineering for Babies & Toddlers

Electronics: CIRCUITS

Mike Roberts, PhD

Lumey

Copyright © 2023 by Michael Roberts
Earthrise Creative, LLC
All rights reserved. No part of this publication may be reproduced, distributed, or transmitted in any form or by any means, including photocopying, recording, or other electronic or mechanical methods, without the prior written permission of the author.
ISBN: 978-1-0882-1268-4

To my two sons Jacob and Caleb. I love how you want to learn about everything around you. Talking to you inspired me to write this book!

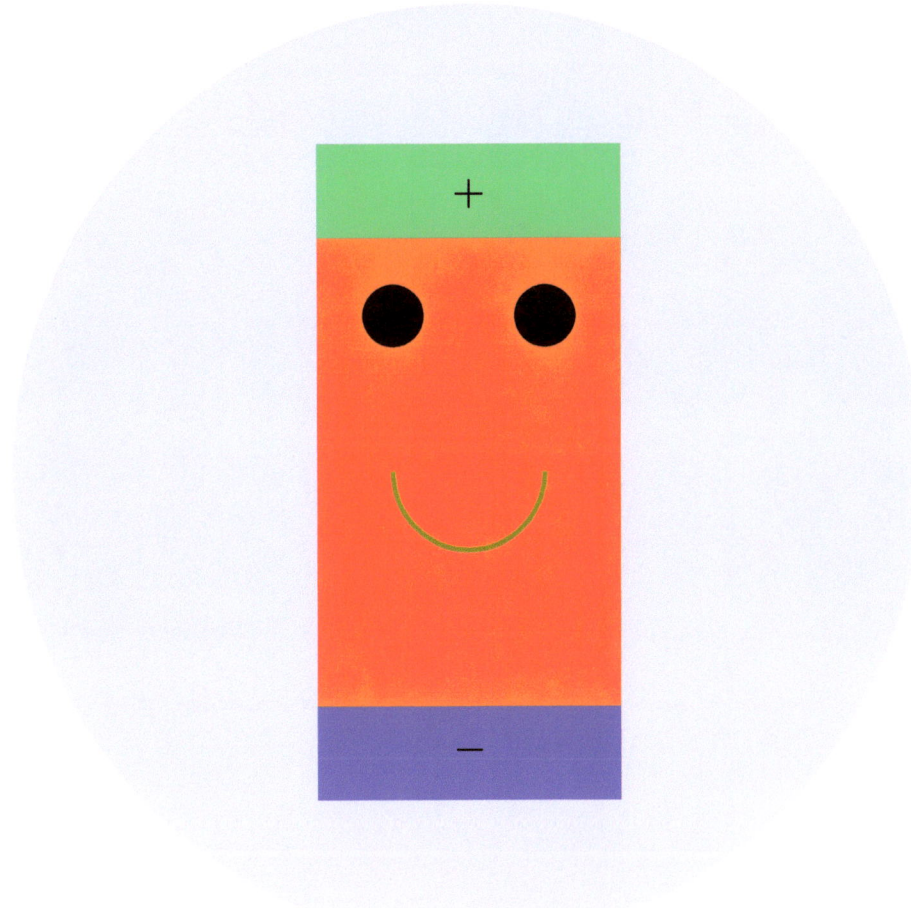

Meet Volty, the Battery! Volty is a red rectangle with a green top and purple bottom. Volty enjoys making new friends and helping them out using his voltage.

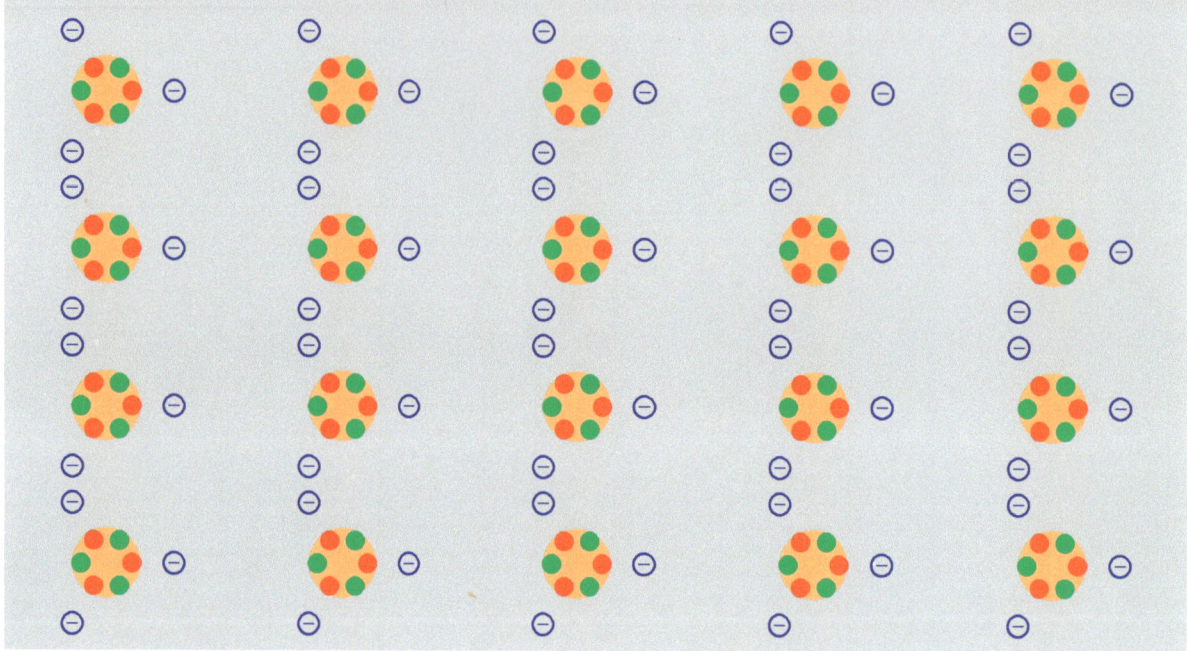

All materials have atoms! Atoms have positive (+) protons, negative (−) electrons and neutral neutrons. Some materials have atoms with free electrons that can move (usually metals). We call these conductors!

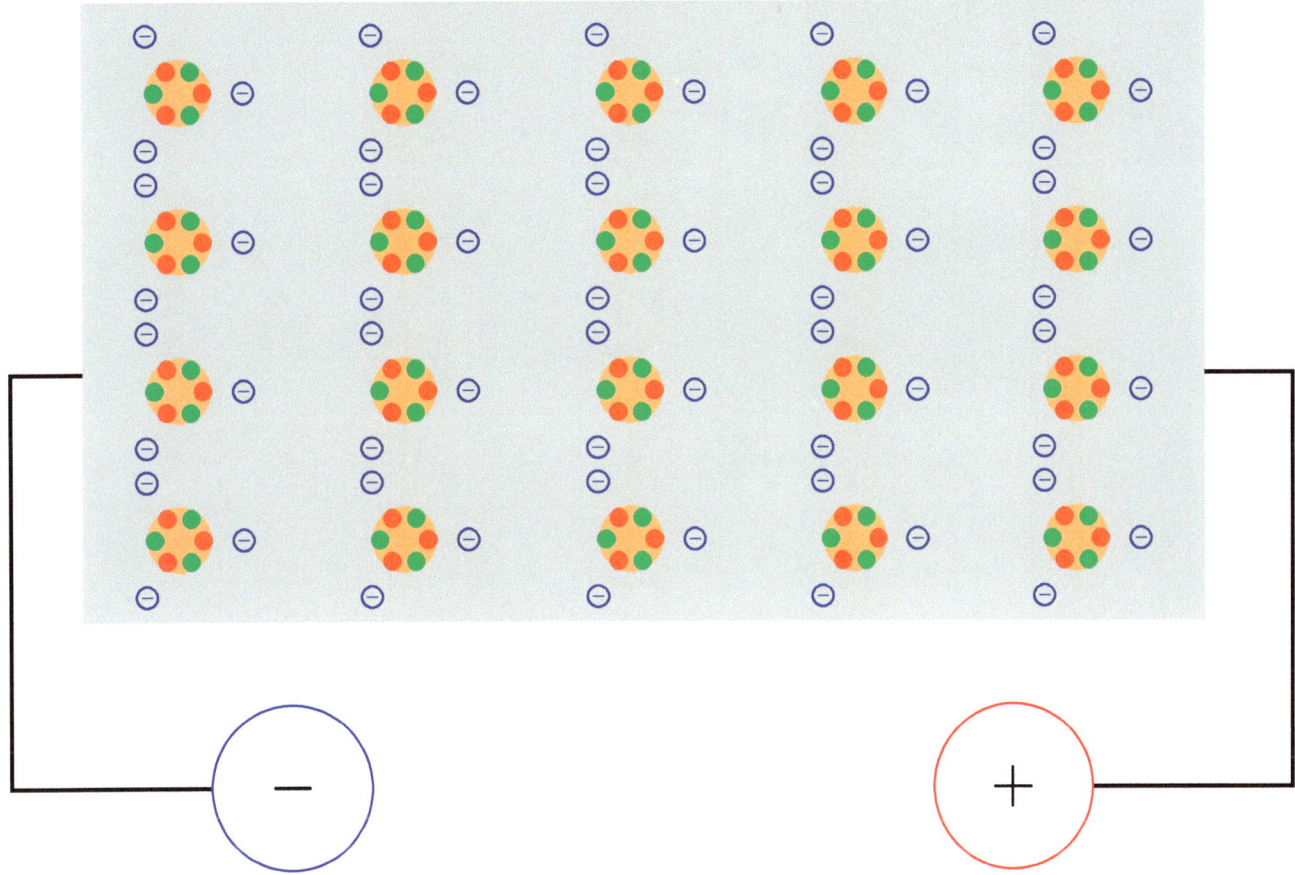

Electrons are attracted to positive charges and repelled by negative charges! What happens if we attach some big positive and negative charges to our conductor through metal wires (shown here as solid black lines)?

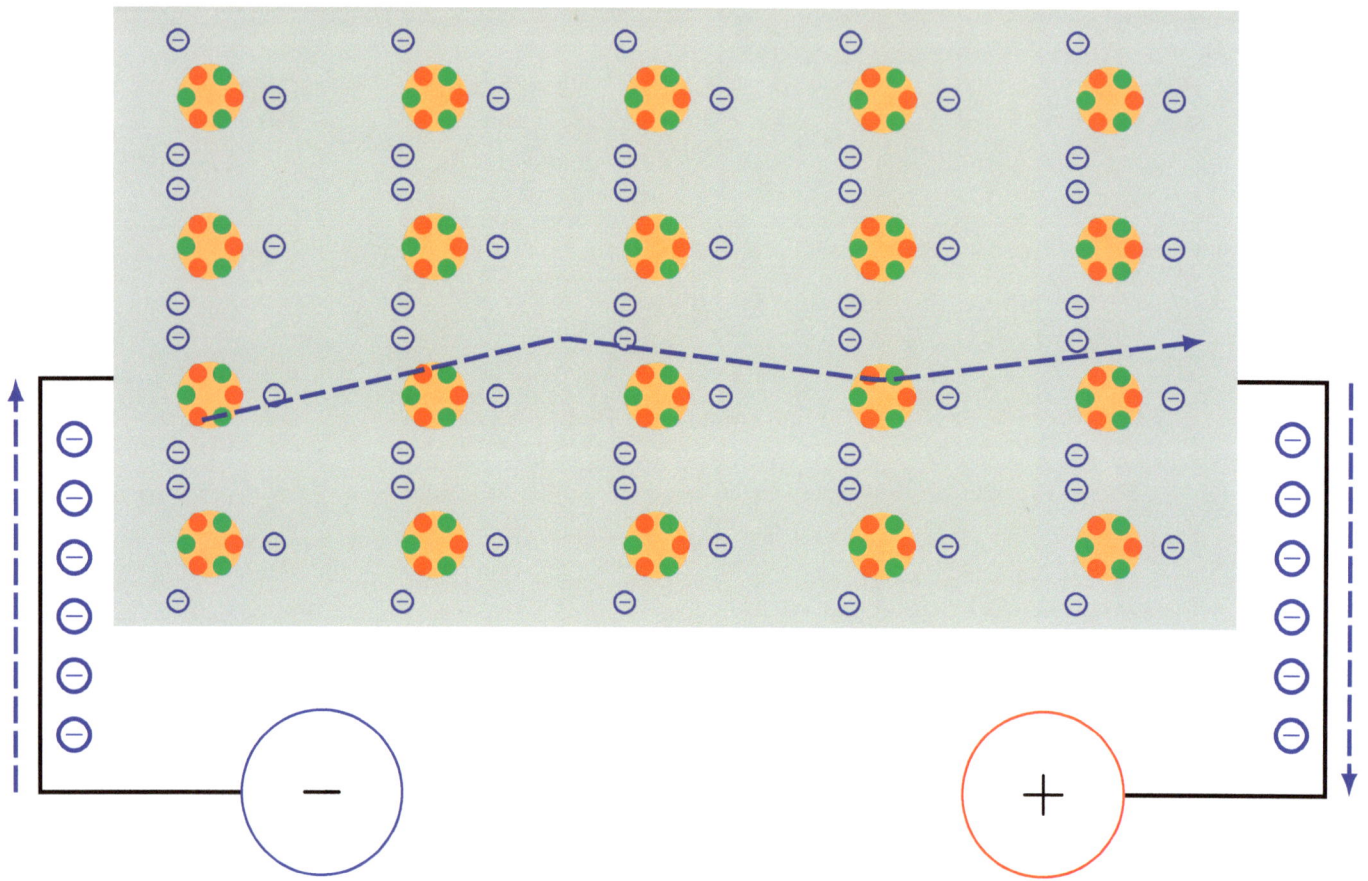

We create a flow of electrons. This is called electric current! We can use this current to do things for us. Here we show the flow of electrons as dashed lines.

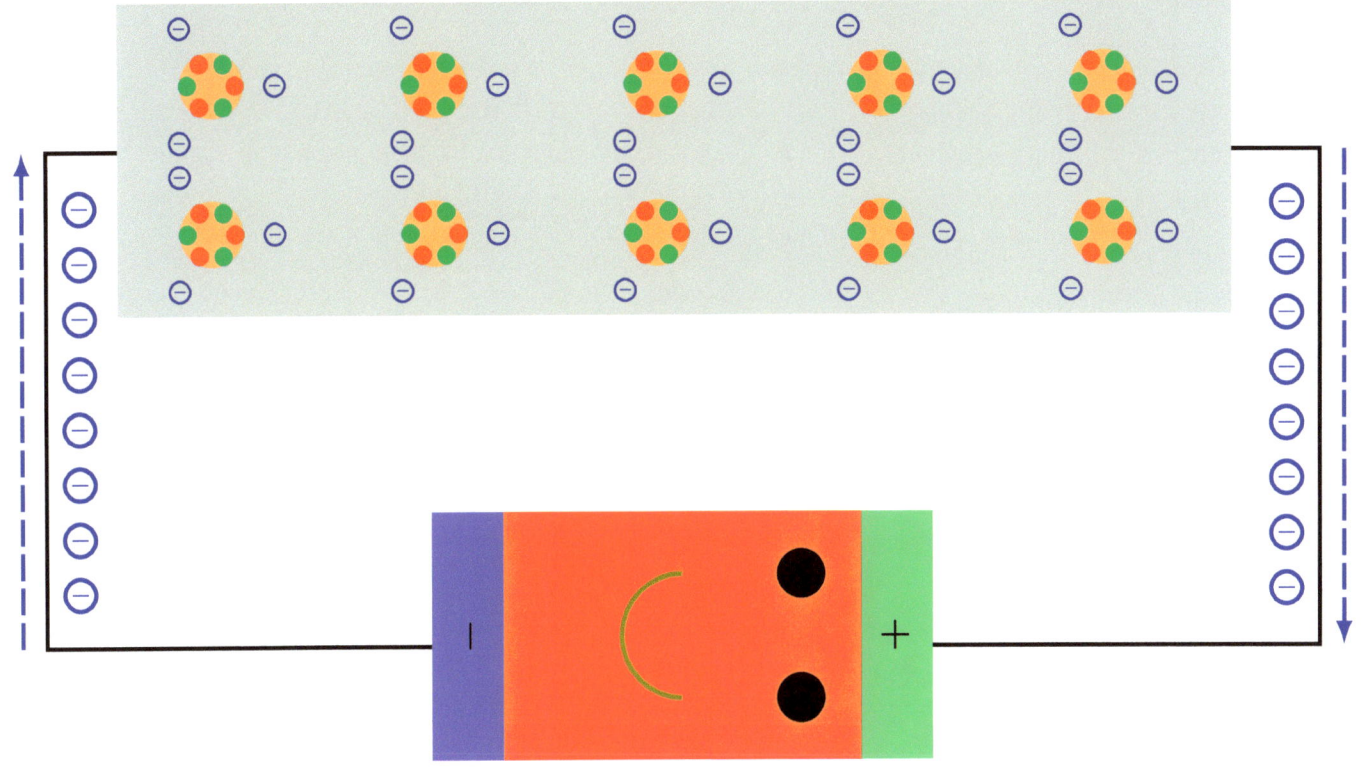

Here we have a thinner conductor. Volty wants to offer us some help! Volty uses his voltage and electron supply to push electrons through.

Here's Lumey the Lightbulb! They have a thin filament that gets hot and glows when you push electrons through. Lumey is incandescent!

Here is a circuit! Volty powers circuits with his voltage. Here he helps his new friend Lumey glow! The electrons flow around the circuit from negative to positive.

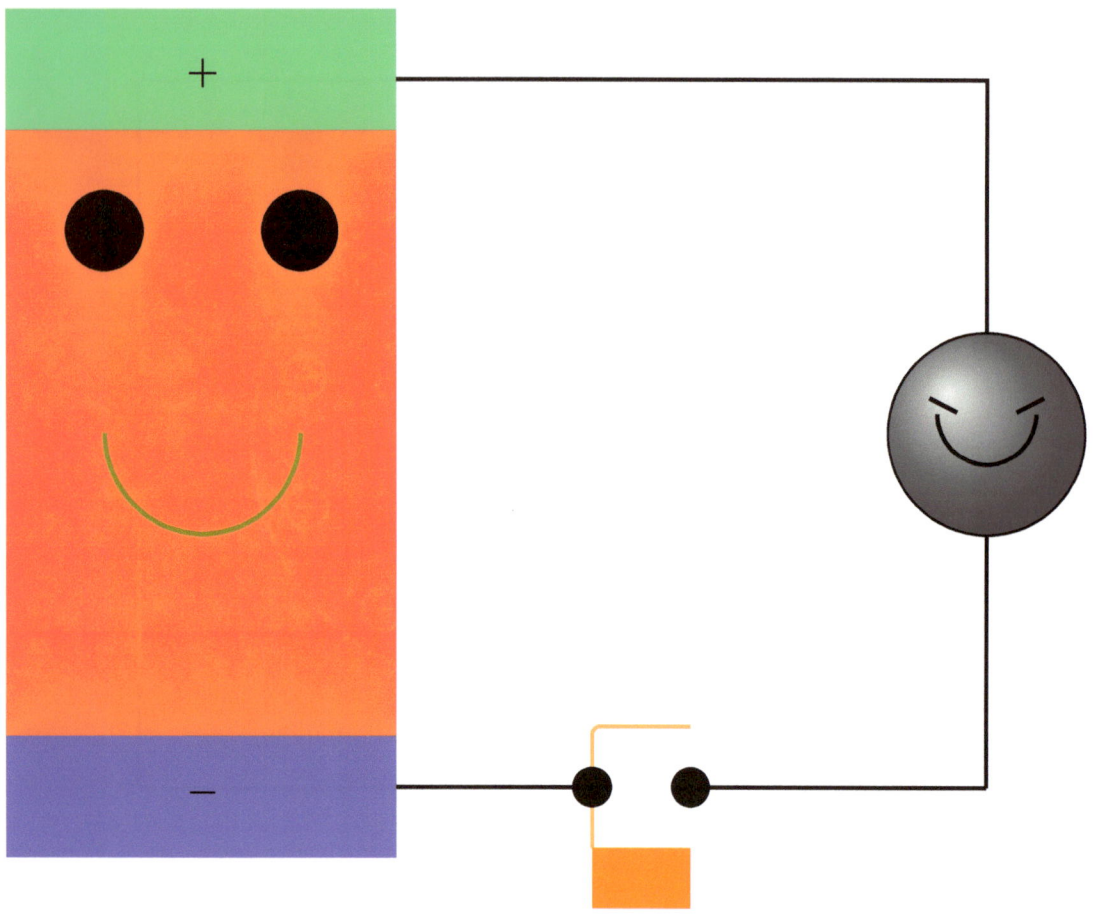

Add a button switch to control the electric current. Here it is not pressed so the wire has a gap - current cannot flow. No current means no light!

We press the button to complete the wire connection. Here the button connects the two wire ends bridging the gap - current flows again. Lumey glows, Yay!

This is a series circuit. Lumey has brought their friend, another incandescent light, to help. The lights are in the same circuit loop! They are one after another in series!

Series circuits share the same current. The current flows through one lightbulb then the other.

Series circuits split the voltage (V).
Each light gets part of the voltage from Volty!
The total voltage across the lights is what Volty shares!

This is a parallel circuit.
The lightbulbs are in separate circuit loops!
They each are connected directly to Volty!

Parallel circuits split the current.
The current from Volty gets divided between the lightbulbs.

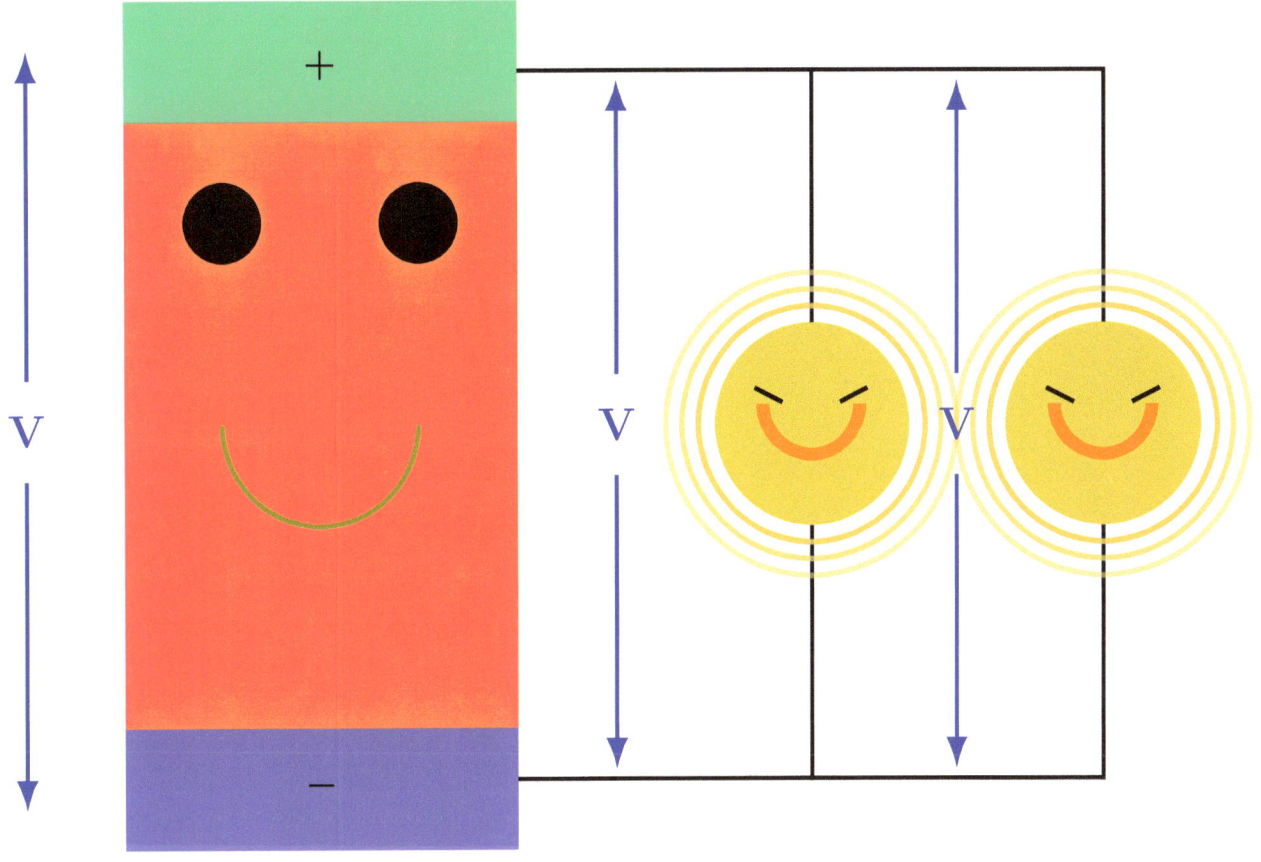

Parallel circuits share the same voltage (V).
Each light gets the same voltage directly from Volty! The voltage across each lightbulb is the same!

With all we have learned we can make even more complicated circuits. Volty is very happy because he now has many friends he can help!

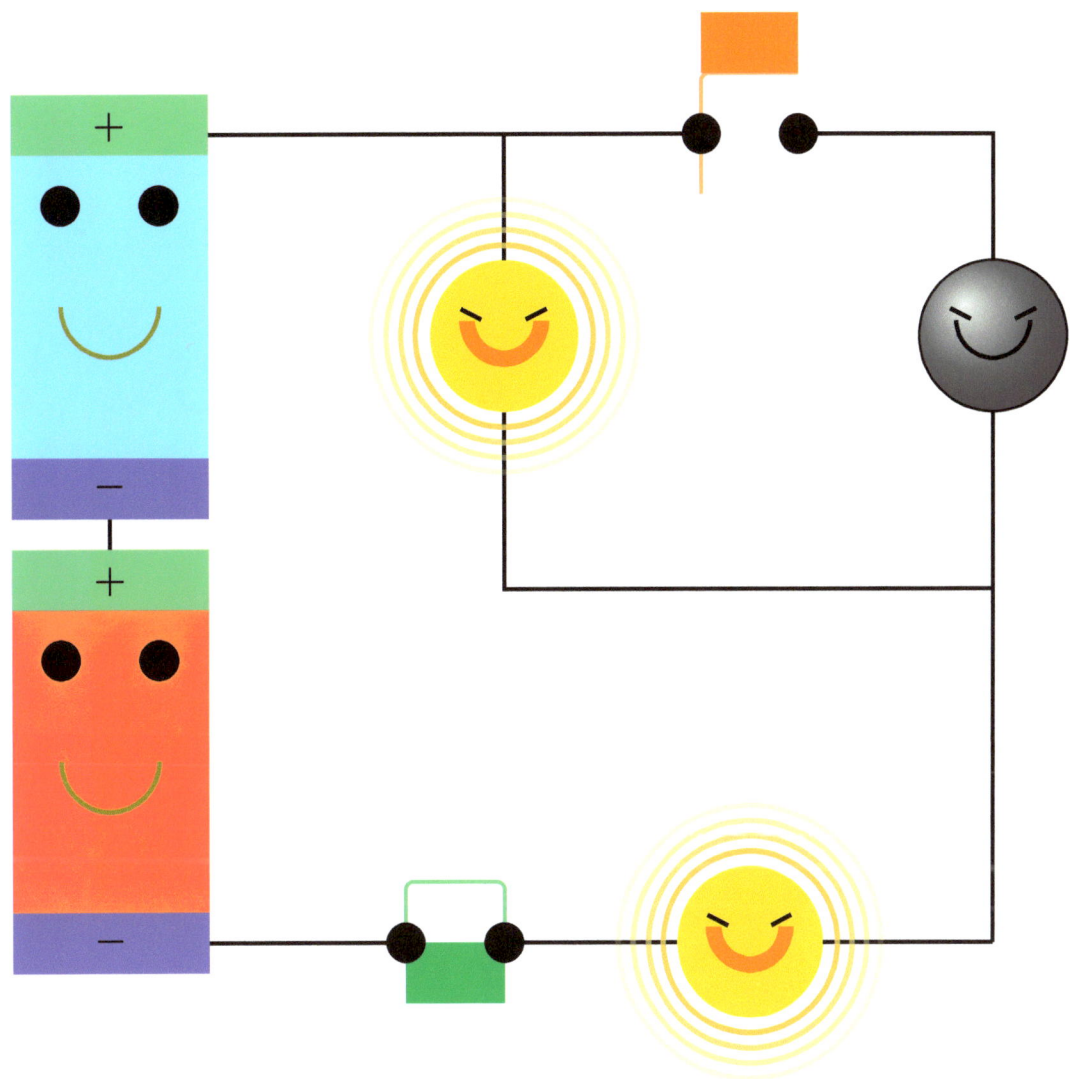

Volty can even get help of his own from his buddy to increase the voltage! See how the brightness increases!

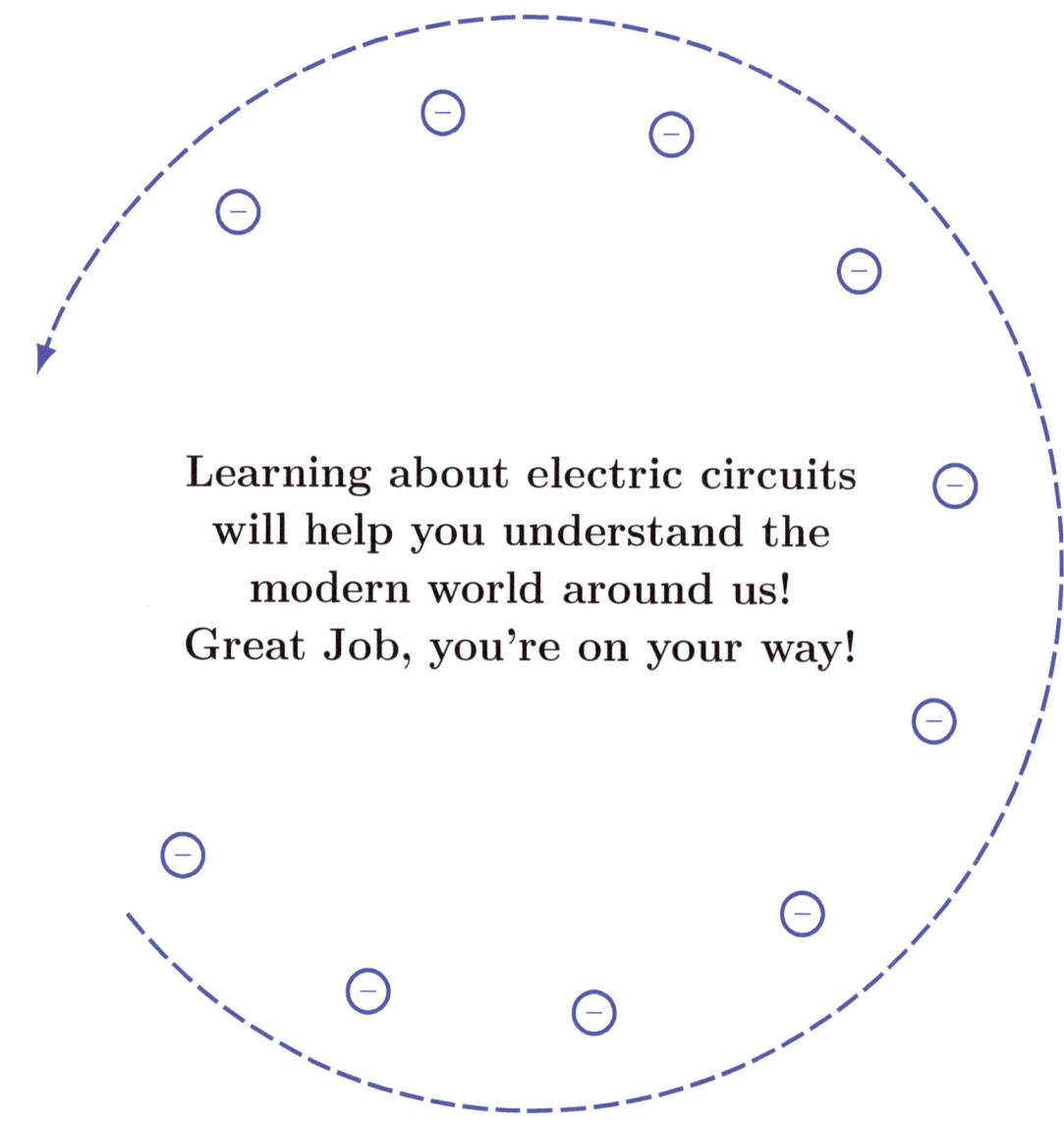

Learning about electric circuits will help you understand the modern world around us! Great Job, you're on your way!

About The Author:

Dr. Mike Roberts earned his PhD in Mechanical Engineering from the University of Arizona in 2012, but he began his engineering journey long before that. He didn't come from a family of engineers, but was always drawn to the field. From an early age, he found joy in dismantling household objects to understand their inner workings, and over time, he mastered the art of repairing and reassembling them.

In his teenage years, Mike began experimenting with electronics, which further fueled his passion for engineering. He pursued his undergraduate studies at NYU-Poly, earning his Bachelor of Science degree in Mechanical Engineering, with a specialization in Mechatronics (a field that synergizes mechanical engineering, electronics, computer science, and robotics). He also completed a minor specialization in electronics.

During his final years at NYU-Poly, Mike developed a fascination for fluid dynamics. Mike had the privilege of spending a summer at NASA's Jet Propulsion Laboratory which fueled his engineering ambition and he realized his academic journey should continue. This pursuit led him to a research assistant position at the University of Arizona, where he conducted both experimental and computational studies on fluid mechanics, specifically focusing on fluid instabilities and turbulent mixing.

As an experimentalist, Mike honed his skills not only from a theoretical perspective, but also through hands-on practical experience. His work encompassed an array of tasks, from soldering electrical circuits and designing then machining parts to writing computer programs for analyzing high-speed camera images of his experiments. Regardless of the task at hand, Mike derived immense joy and pride from his work.

Upon completing his PhD, Mike moved to Oregon, where he now thrives in the tech industry. Here, he also started a family with his wonderful wife. As a father to two young boys, he relishes the opportunity to share his love for engineering, inspiring a new generation to explore the captivating world of STEM.

www.ingramcontent.com/pod-product-compliance
Lightning Source LLC
Chambersburg PA
CBHW041438010526
44118CB00002B/117